What Women Are Saying

"When I went through my divorce, Amethyst helped me understand the importance of allowing God to heal my heart. She provided practical steps to reclaim my life and emphasized the need to trust in God. Her guidance brought clarity and made it possible for me to navigate my journey successfully." — C

"What makes Amethyst Roberson an outstanding therapist is her ability to help you uncover the root causes of your issues. She patiently assists you in understanding these challenges and ultimately conquering them. Her counsel is always infused with God's grace and wisdom, making her support truly transformative." — T

"Healing H.E.R. is a dynamic program that empowers young women to make healthy decisions while fostering both personal and spiritual growth." — J

"Amethyst reassured me that it's okay to not be okay, and that the healing process after losing a loved one takes time. The loss of my husband, who was also my best friend, was devastating, and regaining a sense of normalcy proved more difficult than I anticipated. Thanks to Amethyst's wisdom and compassion, I felt encouraged throughout my journey. I am grateful for her support, as it has made my healing more manageable and filled with hope." — S

HEALING H.E.R.

Discover the Path to Healing, Empowerment & Restoration

By

Amethyst Roberson, MA, LPC

> *"...yet who knows—maybe it was for a time like this that you were made Queen."*
> (Esther 4:14 GNT)

Copyright © 2018 by Amethyst Roberson LLC. First Edition.
224 N. Highway 67 #314, Florissant, MO 63031
Email: office@arrobersontherapy.com

All rights reserved. No part of this book may be reproduced or transmitted in any form or by any means, electronic or mechanical, including photocopying, recording, or by any information storage and retrieval system, without written permission from the author, except in the case of brief quotations in reviews.

Library of Congress Control Number: 2018958097

Published by: **Amethyst Roberson LLC**, a registered publishing entity dedicated to promoting mental health, healing, and empowerment through educational and inspirational content. Printed in the United States of America.

Edited by: Kenkade Publishing (The views expressed within this book are those of the author and do not necessarily represent the views of J. Kenkade Publishing.

ISBN-13: 978-0692191590
ISBN-10: 0692191593

Photography Credit: Hian Oliveira on Unsplash
Cover Design: Md Abir Hasan

Note: This book is designed to serve as a resource for those seeking knowledge on healing, empowerment, and restoration. Readers are advised to seek guidance from a certified relationship coach or licensed counselor before implementing any significant changes in their life. While every effort has been made to ensure the accuracy of the information provided, the author cannot accept responsibility for any errors or differing interpretations of the content. The views expressed in this book are based on personal research and experience and should be considered thoughtfully.

TO THE READERS

This book is for women who are ready to welcome healing into their lives. It is intended for those who are humble and open, willing to seek guidance and rebuild themselves step by step. These pages contain treasures that each woman can discover, integrate into her own life, and share with the people around her.

There is an understanding that the future offers opportunities for healing and restoration for those who choose to actively participate and embrace the roles, expectations, and responsibilities that come with life. Every woman must recognize that certain areas of her life are beyond her control, and that forgiveness is a vital part of the healing process. Other women will also need to address wounds caused by others and those within themselves. Taking responsibility and steering clear of self-sabotage is essential on this journey.

These women do not settle for mediocrity or indifference in their relationships. Instead, they seek meaningful connections and pursue reconciliation. A healed woman embodies characteristics of empowerment, recovery, and restoration.

"Women who invest in Healing H.E.R. will build self-esteem, receive support for goal setting, and gain practical tools to enhance every area of their lives."
— **Amethyst Roberson, MA, LPC, NCC**

DEDICATION

To my mother and best friend Bernice Taylor: Thank you for showing me the essence of being a strong, independent woman and wife. Your teachings and example are treasures I will always hold dear. I love you forever. You are truly missed.

To Robert Taylor: Thank you for being both a father and a friend, offering me wisdom and support to everyone.

To my husband and best friend, Hosea Roberson: Your love, encouragement, and unwavering strength uplift me daily. I am deeply grateful for you and your partnership in this journey. I love you.

To my entire family, pastors, and friends: Thank you for surrounding me with love, guidance, and encouragement. Your support means everything to me.

TABLE OF CONTENTS

To the Readers iii
Dedication v
Facilitator Expectations for Healing H.E.R. 1
Successful Healed Women 3
Expectations for Healing H.E.R. 5
Journey of Growth: Then and Now 7

Building Relationships 13
Session 1: Creating New Values and Beliefs 14
Session 2: Believe God Thinks Well of You 20
Session 3: Perception Is Everything 24
Session 4: What You Allow Will Increase 28
Session 5: Receiving Consolation for Your Soul 31

Assessment 33
Session 6: You Can Solve Whatever Problems You See 34
Session 7: Is Anyone in Need of You? 37
Session 8: Discern Your Encouragers 40
Session 9: Find the Root of Your Pain 42
Session 10: Unpacking Root Issues 44

Formulating Personal and Professional Goals 49
Session 11: You Have What Someone Else Is Missing 50

Session 12: Confidence (Part 1) 54
Session 13: Confidence (Part 2) 57
Session 14: What Is the Source of Your Worth 59
Session 15: Stop Avoiding It! 64

Intervention 67

Session 16: Forget the Past! 68
Session 17: The More You Compromise, the Less Compatible You Are! 73
Session 18: Suitable and Compatible! 80
Session 19: Renewing Your Mind! 82
Session 20: Making Decisions 89

Termination 91

Session 21: Let Go of What Doesn't Change! 92
Session 22: Knowing It by the Fruit! 94
Session 23: The Walk-Through! (Part 1) 96
Session 24: The Walk-Through! (Part 2) 99
Session 25: The Walk-Through! (Part 3) 102

Following Up 105

Session 26: The Walk-Through! (Part 4) 106
Session 27: Follow Up with Favor! 108
Session 28: Admiring vs. Honoring 110
Session 29: Keep Defining Yourself 112
Session 30: Three Keys to Healing H.E.R. 113
References 117

FACILITATOR EXPECTATIONS FOR HEALING H.E.R.

To create a successful and impactful experience for participants in the Healing H.E.R. program, facilitators are expected to:

- **Demonstrate Improvement in Relationships:** Show how healthy interactions can transform lives and foster personal growth.

- **Create a Safe Environment:** Establish a space conducive to open discussions about sensitive topics, where participants feel comfortable sharing their experiences.

- **Utilize Bible-based and Evidence-based Information:** Incorporate teachings that draw from scriptural principles alongside established therapeutic practices.

- **Provide Insight on Celebration:** Encourage participants to celebrate their achievements and the successes of others, fostering a culture of support.

- **Visualize Relationships:** Guide participants in examining their relationships across different timelines—past, present, and future—to identify patterns and growth opportunities.

- **Examine Motives:** Help participants explore their motives and motivations in relationships to foster deeper self-awareness and personal growth.
- **Promote New Communication Strategies:** Teach participants effective communication skills to enhance self-intimacy and connections with others.

SUCCESSFUL HEALED WOMEN

The key qualities necessary for women to heal successfully include:

- **Ability to Rebuild Life:** Women must recognize their worth in God's eyes and be ready to establish a healthy relationship with themselves. They should also be prepared to restore connections with those who have harmed them or to extend forgiveness for past wrongdoings.

- **Readiness for Healing:** Women should determine that this is the right time for their healing journey. They need courage and the capacity to recover, showing resilience, reliability, and realistic expectations.

- **Intentionality:** Successful healing requires deliberate steps toward personal growth. Women should be aware of their self-worth and be ready to face their challenges.

- **Self-Assessment:** Women must assess the damage in their lives and commit to the healing process. This includes a deep love for oneself, letting go of unchangeable circumstances, and being prepared to investigate and intervene in their healing journey.

- **Acknowledgment of Guilt and Shame:** They should learn to manage feelings of guilt and shame to avoid sabotaging their success.

- **Termination of Unhealthy Relationships:** Knowing how to let go of toxic connections is crucial for personal growth and healing.

- **Seek Help:** They must be proactive in seeking assistance to reach their goals, embracing new principles that align with their core values.

Ultimately, a healed woman is empowered, restored, and ready to live authentically, embracing her true self and purpose.

EXPECTATIONS FOR HEALING H.E.R.

Participants in the Healing H.E.R. program can anticipate a transformative experience that focuses on healing, empowerment, and personal growth. The following expectations outline what participants can expect as they embark on this journey:

1. **Commitment to Personal Growth:** Participants should be willing to engage in self-reflection and take responsibility for their healing journey. This includes actively participating in discussions and activities designed to foster growth.

2. **Openness to Change**: An open mindset is crucial for personal transformation. Participants should be ready to embrace new ideas, challenge old beliefs, and consider different perspectives.

3. **Emotional Honesty**: Participants are encouraged to be honest about their feelings and experiences. Sharing in a supportive environment will facilitate healing and connection with others.

4. **Willingness to Explore Trauma**: Understanding and processing past trauma is essential for healing. Participants should be prepared to delve into their past experiences, identify triggers, and work through painful emotions.

5. **Active Participation**: Engaging fully in sessions, completing assignments, and participating in group discussions will enhance the healing experience. Active involvement is key to gaining insights and fostering connections with others.

6. **Support for Others**: Participants should be willing to support their peers throughout the healing process. Building a community of encouragement and understanding is vital for collective growth.

7. **Respect for Confidentiality**: Maintaining the confidentiality of shared experiences is essential to create a safe space for everyone. Participants must honor the privacy of others as they share their journeys.

8. **Focus on Self-Care**: Emphasizing self-care practices throughout the program is crucial. Participants should prioritize their physical, emotional, and spiritual well-being as they navigate their healing journey.

9. **Utilization of Resources**: Participants are encouraged to take advantage of available resources, including readings, support materials, and guidance from facilitators, to maximize their healing experience.

10. **Goal Setting**: Each participant should set clear personal goals for what they hope to achieve through the program. These goals will help guide their focus and efforts throughout the healing process.

By embracing these expectations, participants will cultivate an environment conducive to healing, growth, and empowerment, allowing them to move forward in their lives with renewed purpose and strength.

JOURNEY OF GROWTH: THEN AND NOW

This building relationships section outlines the journey from feeling disconnected and unclear about your values to confidently forming meaningful and healthy connections based on God-centered beliefs and renewed perception.

Chapter Title	Where You Start (Then)	Where You End (Now)
Building Relationships	Unclear values and beliefs, feeling disconnected	Grounded in God-centered values and beliefs, forming healthy relationships
Session 1: Creating New Values and Beliefs	Unsure of your foundational beliefs	Established and aligned with meaningful values
Session 2: Believe God Thinks Well of You!	Doubting God's love and goodness	Confident in God's love and His thoughts toward you
Session 3: Perception Is Everything!	Viewing life through a distorted lens	Seeing life with renewed, positive perception
Session 4: What You Allow Will Increase!	Allowing negative influences to grow	Empowered to nurture positive influences
Session 5: Receiving Consolation for Your Soul	Seeking comfort but feeling unfulfilled	Embracing God's comfort and experiencing peace

This assessment section highlights the progression from feeling powerless to becoming equipped and capable of addressing challenges, understanding your role, and finding clarity and healing.

Chapter Title	Where You Start (Then)	Where You End (Now)
Assessment	Feeling powerless, overwhelmed by problems	Equipped to solve problems and understand your role in the world
Session 6: You Can Solve Whatever Problems…	Feeling powerless over challenges	Empowered with problem-solving skills
Session 7: Is Anyone in Need of You?	Uncertain of your purpose	Aware of your importance in others' lives
Session 8: Discern Your Encouragers!	Surrounded by mixed or harmful influences	Able to identify and cherish true encouragers
Session 9: Find the Root of Your Pain	Struggling with unresolved pain	Acknowledging and beginning to heal your pain
Session 10: Find the Root of Your Pain - Pt 2	Deep pain with no clarity or understanding	Greater clarity and deeper emotional healing

Journey of Growth: Then and Now

This section emphasizes the journey from feeling directionless and insecure to becoming confident, goal-oriented, and secure in your self-worth, ready to achieve both personal and professional aspirations.

Chapter Title	Where You Start (Then)	Where You End (Now)
Formulating Personal and Professional Goals	Feeling inadequate, lacking direction	Confident, motivated, and aligned with your goals
Session 11: You Have What Someone Else Is…	Uncertain of your unique gifts and value	Recognizing your unique contributions
Session 12: Confidence (Part 1)	Struggling with self-doubt	Developing strong, unwavering confidence
Session 13: Confidence (Part 2)	Conditional and fragile self-assurance	Strengthened and resilient confidence
Session 14: What Is the Source of Your Worth	Seeking external validation	Rooted in God's truth as your source of worth
Session 15: Stop Avoiding It!	Dodging difficult truths	Courageously confronting and addressing challenges

This intervention section highlights the transition from being weighed down by the past and unhealthy compromises to living intentionally, with clarity and confidence in your decisions, values, and relationships.

Chapter Title	Where You Start (Then)	Where You End (Now)
Intervention	Carrying unresolved burdens	Free from the past, living intentionally
Session 16: Forget the Past!	Stuck in past memories and regrets	Liberated from the past to embrace the present
Session 17: The More You Compromise…	Settling in ways that hurt you	Refusing to compromise your core beliefs
Session 18: Suitable and Compatible!	Confused about compatibility in relationships	Seeking and recognizing genuine compatibility
Session 19: Renewing Your Mind!	Stuck in old, negative thinking patterns	Transformed and renewed thinking through God's Word
Session 20: Making Decisions	Fearful or indecisive	Making confident, God-led decisions

Journey of Growth: Then and Now

The termination section guides you from holding onto past obstacles and confusion to a place of release and clarity. It focuses on letting go, recognizing fruitful outcomes, and confidently walking through life's challenges.

Chapter Title	Where You Start (Then)	Where You End (Now)
Termination	Holding onto what no longer serves you	Released from what holds you back
Session 21: Let Go of What Doesn't Change!	Struggling to let go of the unchangeable	Released from unhealthy attachments
Session 22: Knowing It by the Fruit!	Confused by mixed outcomes	Discerning what bears good fruit
Session 23: The Walk-Through! (Part 1)	Overwhelmed by life's obstacles	Empowered to walk through challenges with grace
Session 24: The Walk-Through! (Part 2)	Unsure of your path	Confidently moving forward with purpose
Session 25: The Walk-Through! (Part 3)	Feeling stuck in the process	Experiencing progress and momentum

This follow-up section focuses on sustaining the progress you've made. It emphasizes nurturing continuous growth, following up with grace and favor, and using key principles to maintain and deepen your healing journey.

Chapter Title	Where You Start (Then)	Where You End (Now)
Following Up	Uncertain about how to sustain growth and healing	Confident in maintaining and nurturing continuous growth
Session 26: The Walk-Through! (Part 4)	Needing additional support and guidance	Empowered to walk with sustained purpose
Session 27: Follow Up with Favor!	Unsure of how to approach follow-up opportunities	Actively pursuing opportunities with favor and confidence
Session 28: Admiring vs. Honoring	Confused about the difference between admiration and honor	Understanding and applying genuine honor in relationships
Session 29: Keep Defining Yourself	Struggling to maintain a sense of self	Continuously redefining and embracing your true identity
Session 30: Three Keys to Healing H.E.R.	Seeking lasting emotional and spiritual healing	Equipped with tools to heal and empower yourself and others

BUILDING RELATIONSHIPS

SESSION 1

CREATING NEW VALUES AND BELIEFS

For all of us, life begins with a set of principles and values passed down from our parents, grandparents, teachers, and authority figures. These influences shape our foundation and guide our beliefs. Reflect for a moment: what values have you been given? The people in our lives create and mold our world.

This illustration shows a tree diagram where the roots represent your foundational beliefs and values. These roots ground your life and provide stability, while the branches depict how these beliefs grow and shape the outcomes you experience.

Core Values and Beliefs Tree

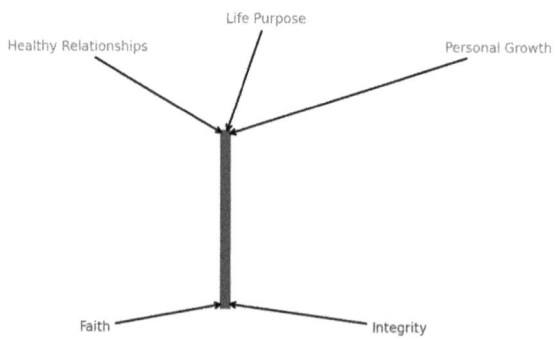

Creating New Values and Beliefs

What common values do you see in your life?

*Reflect and write your thoughts:*_____

_____

_____

The first people who demonstrated values to me were my parents. They were loving, caring, and nurturing. My dad worked as a welder at Chrysler, while my mom worked in a nursing home for most of my childhood. We lived in North County, Saint Louis, MO. My dad later retired early and started his own business. My parents were both seen as leaders in our community, frequently approached for advice and assistance. I looked up to them and admired the values they demonstrated.

I grew up with two brothers, and I was the middle child. My mom often pulled me aside to share wisdom about life, like how to start a bank account or dress appropriately. Those lessons left a lasting impact. We spent a lot of time together as a family, especially at church. While I didn't fully understand everything my parents had endured in their youth, they often shared stories—both humorous and painful—about their experiences.

Despite life's challenges, I never remember missing a meal or hearing my parents argue. They were devoted, walking us to the school bus, packing our lunches, playing with us at the park, standing up for us, and comforting us when we were hurt. They invested time and money to keep us safe and away from the streets. From ages 8 to 18, I participated in both school and summer track, competing in the AAU Junior Olympics and the Missouri State Track Championship. I also played varsity basketball and volleyball, which kept me busy and taught me valuable lessons about dedication and discipline.

Yet, like every family, we faced moments of pain. I recall the profound sadness when my grandmother passed away. She was a strong, church-going woman who adored her family and often made us homemade biscuits. One summer, I watched her cook, never realizing that the pain she later endured was from cancer. The memory of visiting her in the hospital, seeing my warrior grandmother lying in a bed not her own, is etched in my mind. My uncle kissed her with tear-filled eyes, knowing it would be his last time. It was the first time I saw my mother fall to her knees in prayer, pleading with God for strength.

That night shaped my beliefs about family and faith. Watching my mother cry out to God showed me His presence, even in our darkest moments. It created an enduring image of hope and faith for me.

Now, let's shift the focus to you. Think back to your own life, as far as you can remember. Reflect on the moments—both good and bad—that have shaped your values. Recognize that your values are woven into the fabric of your life. While you can't change where your values came from, you can create new ones and break free from patterns that keep you stuck.

Creating New Values and Beliefs

Bring your mind back to the present. Acknowledge the disappointments, detours, and dramas that have occurred. Your future can be greater if you replace negative beliefs with empowering ones. Some memories are worth treasuring, while others you may prefer to forget or have repressed. Still, your current reality is shaped by a script you wrote through these experiences.

The Bible says in Proverbs 23:7, "As a man thinks in his heart, so is he." This verse emphasizes the power of our thoughts. Healing isn't determined by what you've gone through but rather by what you choose to believe now.

This table is designed to help you reflect on your beliefs. In one column, you list old, limiting beliefs that have held you back, and in the other, you write new, empowering beliefs you want to cultivate.

Old Beliefs	New Beliefs
I'm not worthy of love	I am worthy of unconditional love
I must be perfect to be accepted	I am accepted as I am, imperfections and all
I have to handle everything alone	It is okay to seek help and support

COMMITMENT IS KEY

The word "belief" means to commit. What will you commit to in your life? A new relationship? A fresh idea? A financial goal? Don't let past scripts detour you from your purpose. Traumatic experiences—abuse, neglect, or deep hurts—may have left you feeling unworthy. Yet, holding onto these memories only binds you to the pain.

Reflect on your journey and choose whether you will stay committed to the old wounds or commit to healing. If you choose the latter, you activate the promise in Proverbs 23:7. Healing comes when you commit to a new, healthy belief system. Forgiveness clears the heart, and with a clean slate, we can establish new principles to guide our lives.

Remember: What you nurture in your heart will shape your reality. Refuse to let negative thoughts and past hurts dictate your future.

REFLECTION QUESTIONS

1. How do your family values continue to affect you, both positively and negatively?

   _____
   _____
   _____
   _____
   _____
   _____
   _____
   _____
   _____
   _____

2. What challenges have you faced in coping with these values?

   _____
   _____
   _____
   _____
   _____
   _____
   _____
   _____
   _____
   _____

SESSION 2

BELIEVE GOD THINKS WELL OF YOU

I want to encourage you with a principle that has profoundly influenced my life: **You must believe God thinks well of you!**

Despite the strong values my parents and others modeled for me, life's harsh realities still seeped in. I grew up feeling unworthy of God's love and struggled to believe He truly cared for me. As a child, I was intuitive but insecure, hiding my emotions to protect myself. Though I continued talking and playing, I had shut down emotionally.

Unaware of the emotional fortress I had built, I filled my life with self-doubt, guilt, shame, and a need for approval. These negative beliefs were like shaky blocks, holding me together but not allowing me to live up to the expectations instilled in me. I knew I had talents, but fear kept my true, authentic self hidden.

Then, something incredible happened. God noticed me, and I began to feel His presence in a powerful way. As a child, church was a consistent part of my life. One Sunday, during a sermon about faith, I felt overwhelmed by God's presence. Tears threatened to spill, but I held them back, afraid of being seen as weak. The desire to protect myself from rejection ran deep, but this moment marked the start of my journey to Healing H.E.R.

UNDERSTANDING GOD'S LOVE

You need to know—deeply understand—that God thinks well of you. Jeremiah 29:11 reassures us: "For I know the plans I have for you," declares the Lord, "plans to prosper you and not to harm you, plans to give you hope and a future."

How often do we let negative scripts or harmful thoughts about God play in our minds? Perhaps you've wondered, *Can I trust God?* or even *God, why did You let this happen?* These doubts can be obstacles in our faith. But for true healing, we must shift our mindset to believe in God's goodness toward us.

PRACTICAL STEPS TO HEALING

Think of this: God's thoughts toward you are peaceful, not harmful. If a thought is not filled with peace, it's not from God. Imagine how liberating that is! God promises to be upfront and clear: If it isn't peaceful, it isn't from Him.

I've faced doubts, even in my marriage. The fear of not being loved enough haunted me. Yet, in moments of prayer, God revealed to me, *I think well of you. I love you unconditionally.* This became a powerful weapon against any lie that crept into my mind. God's love and care are constant, and He has no doubts about you. Even in times of unforeseen challenges, God reassures us, *I have a plan for you.*

EMBRACE GOD'S PLAN

No matter what you're going through, God promises to bring you through it. Jeremiah 29:11 reminds us that He has a prosperous and hopeful future for us. There's nothing inherently wrong with you; you are enough for God's purpose. Any negativity should be dismissed, replaced with the truth that God speaks well of you.

EXERCISE

Circle and affirm what you believe about yourself. Then live by those beliefs:

- I deserve love
- I am a good person
- I can be trusted
- I can learn to trust myself
- I am fine as I am
- I am worthy
- I can trust my judgment
- It's over now
- I am honorable

- I am lovable
- I can protect myself
- I am safe now
- I am deserving
- I deserve good things
- I can safely show my emotions
- I am fine
- I can be healthy
- I can let it out
- I can make my needs known

(~David Blore Associates Ltd)

SESSION 3

PERCEPTION IS EVERYTHING

This session is crucial because our perception shapes how we feel about ourselves, what we think about ourselves, and how we present ourselves to others and the world.

You may have heard the saying, "Put your best foot forward! First impressions matter!" Indeed, perception is everything. It forms the visible impression we give when we enter a situation and reflects our internal sense of identity. It's essential to let God guide you in understanding who you are and help adjust any distorted perceptions you have—whether they are overly high or too low.

The Apostle Paul often spoke of this balance. He wrote, "When I'm abased, I'm fine; when I am on top of the world, I'm fine" (Philippians 4:12). Paul learned to handle moments of praise, opposition, and indifference by reflecting everything back to God.

This diagram features a house with various windows, each symbolizing a different way you perceive reality. The house represents your sense of self, and each window reflects how your perceptions influence your identity and self-worth.

Perception and Self-Worth House

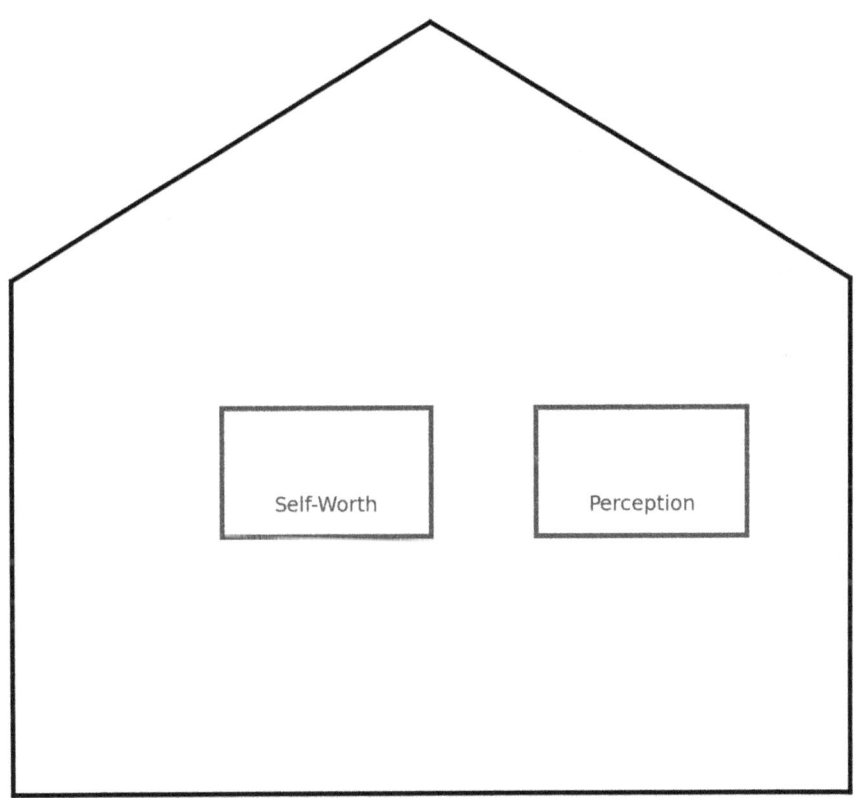

BALANCING SELF-PERCEPTION

Some people struggle with a low perception of themselves, which often manifests as low self-esteem or a poor body image. If this describes you, you may need a confidence boost. Others struggle with managing external validation and praise, leading to inflated self-importance. The Bible encourages balance, as an unbalanced perception leads to inner turmoil. Remember, "perception is a reality," meaning the ideas you hold about yourself shape the reality you live in.

Consider this example: Imagine you live in a house with many windows, and people are looking in from different angles. Each person has a different view and, therefore, a different story about your life. You and your family may have one understanding of your reality inside the house, but others have their unique interpretations based on what they see. This highlights how perception can differ from reality.

YOUR FOCUS SHAPES YOUR PERCEPTION

Your perception is shaped by what you focus on. Is your focus on self-esteem, body image, or the opinions of others? Many people in relationships remain stuck because they can't let go, often due to a lack of forgiveness. Through my work with women—and my personal experiences—I've seen how crucial it is to examine our own self-perceptions.

When I shifted my focus and perception, I could offer better counsel, release people from my past, and even encounter them later in life without emotional turmoil. It wasn't just unforgiveness that held me back but my perception of what I thought should have happened in those relationships. Changing my perspective was key.

A CHALLENGE FOR REFLECTION

If you're struggling with the aftermath of a relationship, I challenge you to explore the meaning of perception. Pray for God to reveal your reality and help you understand your role in past relationships and why they ended. Seek clarity on what you are hyper-focusing on. Perhaps your anger, fear, or hurt stems from something internal rather than the other person.

Ask God to show you which perceptions need to change so your healing can manifest. By shifting your focus, you may find that your perception transforms, opening the way for true healing.

This comparison table contrasts "Distorted Perception" with "Renewed Perception." It highlights how shifts in your thought patterns can lead to an improved self-image and a more accurate understanding of your worth.

Distorted Perception	Renewed Perception
I am not good enough	I am worthy just as I am
Others are always judging me	Others' opinions do not define me
My worth depends on external achievements	My worth comes from within and from God

SESSION 4

WHAT YOU ALLOW WILL INCREASE

There are two key ideas I want to share about this principle. First: **Your life is a result of what you have allowed.**

Let me clarify: I am not minimizing or dismissing trauma or abuse inflicted upon you. If you have suffered abuse—whether sexual, physical, emotional, or through abandonment—it is essential to understand that you did not cause these things. A critical part of healing from abuse is acknowledging that it was not your fault.

Now, once you reach a place of healing, you must take back your life, emotions, and will. It's vital to prevent the pain from festering or being repressed. Ask yourself: *What do I want to increase in my life?* If you don't want the pain to grow, then you must redirect your focus. The things you stop focusing on will eventually lose their hold over you.

FOCUSING ON HEALING

Part of the emotional and spiritual healing process is concentrating on what God calls you to. Sometimes, we continue to dwell on past experiences or relationships that no longer serve us, even though they still affect us. To experience healing, empowerment, and restoration, we must shift our focus from trauma to growth. As we do this, the emotional grip of past hurts will fade.

This principle applies to many areas, even financial health. Often, to receive an increase in our lives, we must let something that no longer serves us die off. Someone once asked me, "How do you move from allowing negative issues to increasing the positive?" My first answer was **establishing boundaries**. You must decide what you will and won't allow in your life, and these decisions should be aligned with God's Word. Sometimes, we carry traditions or habits from our upbringing that aren't biblical or helpful.

PRACTICAL STEPS TO IMPLEMENT THIS PRINCIPLE

1. **Establish Boundaries:** Define what is acceptable in your life based on God's Word.//
2. **Fortify Your Boundaries with Prayer:** Proverbs 18:10 says, "The name of the Lord is a strong tower; the righteous run to it and are safe." There is protection in the boundaries God sets for us.
3. **Shift Your Focus:** Stop dwelling on the negative. What you stop paying attention to will eventually die off.

I remember being in a toxic relationship where someone said, "You'll never get away from me!" That was a wake-up call for me. I had to set boundaries, fortify them through prayer, and realize that God thought well of me and wanted me safe. As my perception changed, the grip of that relationship loosened. Now, I can be in that person's presence without being affected.

TAKE ACTION

Evaluate your life. Recognize the things you've allowed that hinder your productivity and well-being. Start moving away from them. Create a structured plan:

- **Set Boundaries:** Be firm about what you will no longer tolerate.
- **Create a Schedule:** Manage your time effectively.
- **Set Appointments and Deadlines:** Prioritize what matters.
- **Use Resources:** Equip yourself with tools and support to maintain your boundaries.

God is here to help. He desires your safety, timeliness, and excellence as you apply this principle.

SESSION 5

RECEIVING CONSOLATION FOR YOUR SOUL

For this principle, let's reflect on Psalm 94:19: *"In the multitude of my anxieties within me, Your comfort delights my soul."* This session emphasizes receiving God's comfort or consolation for your soul in place of anxiety. The verse highlights the exchange of anxious thoughts for divine peace.

UNDERSTANDING COMFORT AND THE SOUL

Anxiety affects many people in today's world. Although God created us with the ability to feel anxiety as part of our survival mechanism—known as the fight-or-flight response—this response is meant to be temporary. When we experience anxiety frequently and for prolonged periods, our bodies can enter a state of stress and panic, which is unhealthy and can lead to further complications.

Psalm 94:19 acknowledges that anxiety can be overwhelming, but it also reveals that God's comfort is plentiful and can delight our souls. Anxiety often stems from stress, conflict, rejection, loneliness, guilt, loss, or fear of the future. For example, I recall the immense anxiety I experienced when I suddenly lost my mother. The more I dwelled on the loss, the greater my anxiety became. Yet, in those moments, God's comfort offered me relief and delight for my soul.

THE SOURCE OF TRUE COMFORT

God's consolation becomes the ultimate source of relief, replacing other sources of comfort, such as comfort foods, behaviors, or imagined scenarios. Letting go of anxiety isn't always easy, but it's essential to recognize that nothing and no one can replace the unique comfort that God provides.

Understanding the balance between our human reactions and God's command not to be anxious is crucial. It's a battle within our souls, and we must choose to be comforted by God rather than relying on temporary fixes.

ASSESSMENT

SESSION 6

YOU CAN SOLVE WHATEVER PROBLEMS YOU SEE

The guiding scripture for this session is Joshua 1:9: *"Have I not commanded you? Be strong and courageous. Do not be afraid; do not be discouraged, for the Lord your God will be with you wherever you go."*

How many times have we set out with purpose—whether for God, a spouse, a friend, or family—only to feel discouraged? Sometimes, it's God Himself giving us the encouragement we need to keep going. Self-doubt can blind us to the fact that we have what others need and that we are uniquely equipped to solve problems.

This principle emphasizes that **you can solve whatever problems you see.** To do so, you need confidence. With confidence, you can complete any mission God assigns or any task entrusted to you by those you care about. Problem-solving is intricately tied to your purpose.

IDENTIFYING YOUR PURPOSE THROUGH PROBLEMS

Consider this: Do you want to understand your current place in life? Look at the problems you notice around you. The problems you are drawn to solve are directly connected to your purpose. Your purpose is always meant to intersect with a problem that needs addressing.

By evaluating where you are on your journey and identifying the problems that resonate with you, you can better discern your purpose. Confidence in your abilities is crucial as you work toward your goals.

THE PATH TO PROMOTION

Promotion comes from solving problems. Reflect on any promotion you've earned or desired; it likely required effort and problem-solving on your part or that of a group or community. Promotion represents growth—sometimes a vertical move and sometimes a horizontal one. Sometimes, it means moving away from toxic relationships or unhelpful situations to something more aligned with your purpose.

How do you leave a relationship that is more harmful than beneficial? Through promotion, which comes from solving problems and aligning with your God-given purpose. You are called to be a problem solver in the lives of those around you. This doesn't mean enabling others or trying to fix everything, but rather using your talents and abilities as answers to the challenges people face.

Problems aren't always negative or monumental. Sometimes, solving a problem means offering an encouraging word or providing energy and support, even if it's just for a season.

YOUR GIFTS ARE MEANT TO BE USED

Your gifts and talents are not only tools for personal success but also blessings from God meant to uplift the world around you. A gift is a divine favor, and you may not be using it to its fullest potential. Or, perhaps, you've used your gifts but haven't seen the impact you expected. I urge you to connect your gifts to the problems you observe. When you use your talents to address those problems, you will see growth and promotion in your life.

SESSION 7

IS ANYONE IN NEED OF YOU?

Evaluate your life, skills, and talents by asking yourself: *Is anyone in need of me—of who I am and who God says I am? Do I have the ability to solve a problem in someone's life?*

This principle comes from a personal reflection. For instance, if I claim to be a counselor but no one ever seeks me for counseling, life coaching, or any form of help, I must assess the situation. Am I walking in the purpose I believe is meant for me? I'd need to consider:

- Have I marketed myself effectively?
- Did I clarify my purpose and goals?
- Have I shared the right information?
- Did I create brochures or promotional materials?

It's also crucial to consider whether you're in the right time and season for your calling. If you've done all you can to make yourself marketable and confident in your purpose but still haven't seen results, it might be time to reassess.

A CHALLENGE FOR SINGLE WOMEN

I want to specifically challenge single women to reflect on this: *Is anyone in need of who you are right now?* There was a time in my life when I felt I had little to offer. I wasn't ready to be a "helpmeet" as the Bible describes, because I was spent, torn, and broken.

If you feel you're in a broken place, ask yourself, "Is anyone in need of me in this state? Can anybody use the pain and hurt I carry?" If the answer is "No," it's important to work through these principles to facilitate healing. Once healed and walking in your healing, you'll be able to offer emotional and spiritual support to others.

Single women, consider this: *Beyond your physical self, is your spiritual self ready to be needed?* If you presented the spiritual version of yourself to a potential partner, would he find value in who you truly are? Remember, when you get married, your authentic self will emerge. Make sure that your spiritual self is strong enough to uplift and support your partner.

A CHALLENGE FOR MARRIED WOMEN

Marriage involves a continuous process of self-assessment. The qualities we bring as wives aren't something we start only when we marry—they are ongoing. And yes, men must bring and maintain their contributions as well!

SELF-REFLECTION AND GROWTH

I encourage all women to reflect deeply on this session's question: *Is anyone in need of who you are today?* If not, it may be time to adopt new principles. By understanding your belief system, building confidence, and removing any negative perceptions, you'll be better equipped to solve problems.

A spouse or future spouse will look for a partner who can support and help solve life's challenges, just as you will look for someone who can do the same for you. So, assess and diagnose where you stand. This self-awareness will make you stronger and more prepared for meaningful connections.

SESSION 8

DISCERN YOUR ENCOURAGERS

The principle for this session is: **Discern your encouragers!** This concept is crucial and one I continually revisit to understand who God has placed in my life to uplift me, especially in each season.

While this session may sound self-focused, it's essential for your well-being. We all need someone to turn to for genuine encouragement. The Bible provides numerous examples of encouragers, and the Apostle Paul often expressed his joy and excitement over those who came to lift him up and support him.

THE IMPORTANCE OF ENCOURAGERS

As women, we often give so much of ourselves without receiving the nurturing and care we need. Yet, having encouragers is vital for our balance and growth in various roles, including womanhood, motherhood, and our professional lives. Paul's example reminds us that we all need support to thrive.

Proverbs 15:22 says, *"Plans fail for lack of counsel, but with many advisers, success is wrought."* Think about your plans for this season—whether it's a personal goal like weight management or a professional ambition. This verse encourages us to seek out those who can guide and inspire us.

HONOR AND ADMIRATION

It's important to differentiate between those you admire and those you honor. Admirers provide inspiration and information. In contrast, people you honor are those you look up to, and they can pour back into your life. Look for encouragers who can reciprocate and invest in your growth and well-being.

Proverbs 24:6 says, *"Surely, you need guidance to wage war, and victory is won through many advisers."* This wisdom is a reminder of the importance of seeking out and discerning encouragers. Whether you need guidance in an unhealthy relationship, career challenges, or personal goals, success often comes through the counsel of trusted advisers.

FINDING YOUR ENCOURAGERS

Proverbs 11:14 states, *"In the multitude of counsel, there is wisdom."* Remember that encouragers don't always have to be people; they can be books, podcasts, or even television shows that offer wisdom and life-changing insights.

So, discern your encouragers wisely. Seek out those who can truly uplift and guide you on your journey.

SESSION 9

FIND THE ROOT OF YOUR PAIN

The guiding scripture for this session is Psalm 139:23-24: *"Search me, O God, and know my heart; test me and know my anxious thoughts. See if there are any offensive ways in me and lead me in the way everlasting."*

Let's focus on the phrase *"offensive ways."* This scripture invites God to heal us from deep hurts—pains that have knocked the wind out of us. The psalmist is asking God to examine their thoughts, anxieties, and the pains that have left lasting wounds.

You may be dealing with pains from the past, fears about the future, or current worries that feel overwhelming. This prayer to God is a heartfelt plea: *Lord, look deep within me. You know my faults, my fears, and my heart. Reveal the things that have wounded me so I can find healing.*

IDENTIFYING YOUR PAIN

The phrase *"search me"* means to thoroughly examine or investigate. God is invited to reveal the sources of our distress and begin the healing process. *Anxious thoughts* refer to those fears that multiply and consume us, making us apprehensive about the future. These may stem from past offenses, betrayals, or situations that have caused harm.

Finding the root of your pain involves recognizing the multiplying negative thoughts that lead to your distress. Once you identify these, you can pray: *Lord, search me, reveal my faults, and show me any painful ways that I have been carrying. Help me to stop offending myself and to heal from the offenses of others.*

THE PROCESS OF HEALING

Remember, I'm not suggesting that you relive past traumas or force yourself into discomfort. However, a thoughtful and honest self-assessment is a crucial first step toward healing. Understanding the root of your pain allows you to address it and find lasting peace.

SESSION 10

UNPACKING ROOT ISSUES

In this session, we explore the deep roots that contribute to our emotional struggles, including trust issues, control, codependency, and rejection. These roots often stem from unhealed trauma, unresolved feelings, or unmet emotional needs, and they can significantly impact our overall well-being.

Trust Issues

Definition: Trust is the reliance on someone or something. It is essential for society's functioning and our happiness. Without trust, fear takes over.

Signs of Trust Issues:

- Difficulty forming close friendships or relationships
- Doubts that interfere with intimacy or closeness
- Turbulent or dramatic relationships
- Anxiety around loved ones
- Fear of physical closeness
- Believing others are deceitful or malicious without evidence

Origins of Trust Issues: Trust issues often start in childhood, influenced by inadequate care, neglect, or abuse. Experiences like betrayal, social rejection, or being let down by others can damage our ability to trust. These issues can also be amplified by traumatic events in adulthood, such as illness, loss, or physical harm.

Addressing Trust Issues: Recognize that you are not alone. With guidance, you can rebuild trust, enhancing your relationships and overall sense of well-being.

Control Issues

Definition: Control is exerting influence over our environment or others. It can become unhealthy when it stems from fear or the need to feel secure.

Causes: Control often arises from traumatic experiences that left us feeling powerless. People who struggle with control may micromanage or establish rigid rules to regain a sense of safety.

Signs of Control Issues:
- Lack of trust
- Anxiety and fear of losing control
- Compulsive behaviors or perfectionism
- Emotional sensitivity and avoidance of painful feelings

Healing from Control Issues: Therapy can help uncover the fear driving the need for control. Recognizing this self-defensive behavior allows for growth, self-compassion, and developing healthy coping strategies.

Exercise: Identify the benefits of releasing control. List your strengths and develop an action plan to use your talents for meaningful activities rather than trying to control everything.

Codependency

Definition: Codependency is prioritizing others' needs over your own. It often leads to unhealthy, imbalanced relationships where you seek validation by helping or saving others.

Signs of Codependency:

- Low self-esteem and a sense of shame
- Difficulty setting boundaries
- A need to "save" or protect loved ones
- Ignoring personal needs and well-being
- Obsessive desire to appear independent and competent

Origins of Codependency: Often rooted in childhood, codependency can arise from feeling neglected or unimportant. This leads to a belief that your needs are secondary and only others' happiness matters.

Exercise: List the advantages of living independently from others' approval. Identify your strengths and talents, and set goals for building a life that honors your needs and desires.

Rejection

Rejection leaves a lasting impact, often originating from close relationships. A significant example from my experience was a young girl in our youth ministry who shared the pain of her father's rejection, which had a profound effect on her sense of worth and belonging.

Impact of Rejection: Rejection affects our need for love, security, acceptance, and identity. Many people experience rejection from parents, partners, or peers, leading to long-lasting emotional scars.

Healing from Rejection

Steps for Processing Rejection:

1. Describe your experience in detail, including your age, the setting, and who was involved.
2. Reflect on how this rejection has shaped your life.
3. Identify the emotions tied to the event.
4. Recall the event in a safe environment, without being overwhelmed by negative thoughts or feelings.

SHARING YOUR PAINFUL MEMORIES

It's normal to want to avoid painful memories. However, avoiding trauma only intensifies its negative effects. When the time feels right and safe, share your experience with a trusted person or professional. Healing begins when we face our pain head-on.

Assignment: Describe your rejection experience in as much detail as possible, and reflect on similar events in your life. Identify harmful coping mechanisms you've used and consider healthier ways to address your emotional wounds.

FORMULATING PERSONAL AND PROFESSIONAL GOALS

SESSION 11

YOU HAVE WHAT SOMEONE ELSE IS MISSING

It's vital to enter any group or community with confidence, knowing that you bring something valuable. Whether it's information, experience, wisdom, or knowledge, be assured that you have something to contribute. This confidence is crucial because life often throws negativity your way, testing your resolve when you're trying to be an encourager, professional, or simply working on personal goals.

Many situations and people may try to shake your confidence, fill you with fear, or make you doubt your worth. That's why it's so important to be grounded in the knowledge of your unique contributions. You deserve to be celebrated. Surrounding yourself with people who uplift and respect you helps filter out negativity and enhances your integrity and reputation.

SURROUND YOURSELF WITH SUPPORTIVE PEOPLE

For your personal and professional goals, it's crucial to be around individuals who will celebrate your achievements. This support network will not only affirm your efforts but may also open new opportunities through meaningful connections.

Throughout this book, we've explored concepts like creating new beliefs, understanding that God thinks well of us, managing our perceptions, and realizing that what we focus on grows. We've discussed how to comfort ourselves, solve problems, and discern our encouragers. We've also dug deep into identifying the root causes of our pain and how to begin the healing process.

Now, it's time to think beyond ourselves. You have what someone else is missing, and it's your duty to share your wisdom and experiences to help others. Healing, empowerment, and restoration—these are the foundations of this journey, not just for you but also for those around you.

FINDING YOUR "WHY"

Reflecting on my own life, I realized that my "why" was connected to my passions: what made me angry, what kept me awake at night, and what brought me joy. Your "why" is often wrapped up in your "what"—what drives you, excites you, and moves you to take action. God has given each of us unique gifts and talents meant to bless our families and communities.

Take some time to create a list of what compels you and brings you joy. This list can be a guide to discovering your purpose. Your passion is your knowledge ignited! Don't let your gifts remain untapped—use them to make an impact. As I pursued my calling, holding onto God's purpose, I found my voice and passion, which became vehicles for God's glory.

SERVING OTHERS WITH PURPOSE

One pivotal moment for me was when I had a vision of helping young women, specifically those aged 12 to 21. This vision clarified my purpose, and I committed myself to learning and growing, serving others with all my heart. My experiences, including volunteering in youth ministry and learning from mentors, showed me that service is a key that unlocks doors to great partnerships.

Remember, saying "yes" to what reveals itself as your purpose is essential. Everything you've been through is preparing you for this moment. Trust that God is for you, not against you. Speak confidently, take action, and show others how to move forward and thrive. Be a problem-solver and support others in overcoming life's challenges.

THE POWER OF GIVING

A great mentor once told me, "Sowing is the key to growing." Invest your time, talent, and treasure in others. I witnessed this principle through my parents, who lived generously and were blessed in return. You have what someone else is missing, and when you commit to improving yourself and helping others, you create a ripple effect of grace and significance.

Do not give up now. Don't dwell on who you used to be but focus on who you are becoming. Embrace this new way of living, filled with unlimited grace and purpose.

SESSION 12

CONFIDENCE (PART 1)

Let's begin this session with Hebrews 10:35: *"Therefore, do not cast away your confidence, which has great reward. For you need endurance so that after you have done the will of God, you may receive the promise."*

UNDERSTANDING CONFIDENCE

Confidence is an internal trust and closeness with yourself. It is the feeling or belief that you are capable of accomplishing whatever you set your mind to. Sometimes, it feels like God is actively assisting us, while at other times, it may seem like He has left us to figure things out on our own. Regardless of the season you're in—whether you're struggling to make things work or everything seems to be flowing easily—confidence is essential. You need a steadfast belief in your abilities and the conviction that you can achieve your goals.

Hebrews 10:35 emphasizes the importance of confidence. The writer is telling us not to cast it away because it brings great rewards. These rewards often come in the form of personal promotion or advancement. Before any significant breakthrough or graduation in life, your confidence lays the foundation for feeling good about yourself and your decisions. This self-assuredness gives you the endurance needed to accomplish God's will.

THE REWARDS OF CONFIDENCE

Confidence not only makes you feel good about your choices but also opens the door to endurance. Endurance, in turn, leads to greater rewards and opportunities for promotion. Whether you're navigating the end of a long-term relationship, feeling stuck, or seeking a new direction, building your confidence is crucial. Believe in your calling and what God has prepared for you. With this confidence, you'll be ready to move forward, opening doors to new opportunities that align with your destiny.

BUILDING CONFIDENCE THROUGH CONSISTENCY

Think of confidence as the consistent practice of certain habits or actions. By repeatedly doing things that strengthen your confidence, you'll start producing new, positive behaviors. This consistency helps push out harmful or distracting habits, leading to a process of transformation. It's vital for the people you're called to help to recognize and appreciate your authenticity and gifts. You don't need their jealousy; you need their genuine support and celebration.

You'll know people celebrate you when they respect your words, talents, and contributions. In forming your professional and personal goals, surround yourself with those who honor and respect your journey. You cannot have a healthy relationship with someone who doubts your worth or fails to acknowledge the value of your calling.

LETTING GO OF THOSE WHO DON'T SUPPORT YOU

If people in your circle don't believe in or respect your purpose, don't waste energy trying to change their minds. Their approval isn't necessary for you to fulfill your destiny. Focus on your path and trust that, in time, the right people will come into your life—those who are convinced and uplifted by your presence and purpose.

SESSION 13

CONFIDENCE (PART 2)

Let's begin with John 10:10: *"The thief does not come except to steal, to kill, and to destroy. I have come that they may have life, and that they may have it more abundantly."*

In this scripture, Jesus clearly defines His purpose in our lives and contrasts it with the enemy's purpose. The enemy's aim is to steal, kill, and destroy, while Jesus came to offer us an abundant life. As we explore confidence further, let this be a reminder of the promise we have in Him.

REFLECT ON YOUR CONFIDENCE CHALLENGES

Think about this: What is the worst insult someone has ever thrown at you? How did it impact your confidence and hold you back, either then or now? Reflecting on this can help you identify limiting beliefs you've accepted about yourself. Remember, with God, there are no limits to what we can achieve. So, what beliefs or labels have restricted you?

When you begin to build your confidence, expect opposition—even from unexpected places, such as family, friends, or colleagues. The enemy may use people or situations to steal your dreams and diminish your self-worth. Prepare your heart and mind to face these challenges, keeping your focus on the abundant life Jesus promised.

IDENTIFY AND RELEASE LIMITING BELIEFS

Consider the areas in your life where your confidence has been shaken. Maybe a broken relationship shattered your dreams, or perhaps you're holding on to past hurts or an idea of what life "should" be. Write down the names of people or the specific events that have impacted you. Assess whether these influences have been positive or devastating to your growth.

If you discover deep wounds that require healing, seek Godly counsel or additional resources to support your journey. Remember, confidence in Christ is unshakeable, and He desires for you to live a life filled with purpose and abundance.

SESSION 14

WHAT IS THE SOURCE OF YOUR WORTH

What is the true source of your worth? Let's reflect on this question through the lens of *The Five Love Languages* by Gary Chapman. According to Chapman, the five love languages are gifts, words of affirmation, acts of service, quality time, and physical touch. These love languages are foundational in shaping our sense of worth. However, when these foundations are unbalanced or neglected, it can lead to a distorted view of love and self-worth.

This imbalance often manifests as negative self-perception, affecting how we remember and interpret our life stories. For instance, someone who craves quality time but was deprived of it during childhood may feel abandoned or unworthy. Similarly, someone who receives gifts but lacks genuine affirmation may never feel truly loved or satisfied. Reflect on whether a lack of one of these love languages has hindered your healing or sense of self-worth.

RECOGNIZING THE IMPACT

Understanding how these love languages influence us is crucial, especially when pursuing personal or professional goals. Challenges in the workplace, relationships, or marriage can trigger deep-seated emotions tied to unmet needs. When others fail to respond to you in your primary love language, it can evoke feelings of inadequacy or rejection.

It's essential to evaluate your self-worth, how you perceive yourself, and how this perception influences your actions and relationships. Look at your worth through the lens of God's Word. Remember, no love language or human connection can completely fill the void in another person's life. Only God can be the true source of your worth and identity.

Evaluating your self-worth involves self-reflection, understanding your values, and acknowledging your intrinsic value beyond external achievements or validation. Here are some steps to guide you:

1. Reflect on Your Core Beliefs

- Ask yourself: *What do I believe about myself, both positively and negatively?*
- Identify any limiting beliefs that might be holding you back. Write them down and challenge their validity.

- Replace negative thoughts with affirmations based on your true worth, not on what you achieve or how others perceive you.

2. Recognize Your Intrinsic Value

- Understand that your worth isn't tied to your accomplishments, appearance, or social status.
- Acknowledge that you are valuable simply because you exist. Your worth is not something you have to earn or prove.

3. Identify Your Strengths and Talents

- List your skills, strengths, and things you do well. These could be personal traits like compassion or abilities such as problem-solving.
- Reflect on moments when you used these strengths to make a positive impact.

4. Examine Your Values

- Identify what matters most to you. Is it family, honesty, creativity, or service to others?
- Evaluate whether your daily actions align with these core values. Living in alignment with your values can boost your sense of self-worth.

5. Consider the Five Love Languages

- Reflect on how you give and receive love (gifts, words of affirmation, acts of service, quality time, physical touch). Are your needs being met in healthy ways?
- Consider how unmet needs in these areas have influenced your self-worth and how you can seek healing.

6. Set Boundaries

- Recognize that valuing yourself means setting boundaries to protect your time, energy, and well-being.
- Practice saying "no" when necessary and honor your own needs as much as you honor others'.

7. Seek Affirmation Through God's Word

- Meditate on scriptures that affirm your value, such as Psalm 139:14: *"I am fearfully and wonderfully made."*
- Remind yourself that your worth comes from being a child of God, loved unconditionally.

8. Celebrate Your Achievements

- Take time to acknowledge and celebrate your accomplishments, big or small. Reflect on how far you've come, and be proud of your progress.
- Focus on growth rather than perfection.

9. Practice Self-Compassion

- Be kind to yourself when you make mistakes. Remember, no one is perfect, and setbacks are part of the growth process.

- Speak to yourself with the same kindness and understanding that you would offer a friend.

Final Thoughts

Self-worth is a journey of recognizing your inherent value, apart from external validation. It requires self-awareness, self-compassion, and a focus on what truly matters to you. Remember, your worth is constant and unwavering, rooted in who you are, not in what you do.

Would you like to dive deeper into any of these steps or need more guidance on a specific area?

SESSION 15

STOP AVOIDING IT!

In this session, we're diving into the topic of avoidance. What is the *"it"* in your life? Is it a person, a situation, a task, or even a place you've been avoiding like the plague? Is it a difficult conversation you need to have or an unresolved issue that's holding you back?

UNDERSTANDING AVOIDANCE

We often avoid things for many reasons, and this ties directly into our confidence. When your confidence is rooted in who you are and in God's purpose for your life, you must also embrace the boldness He gives you. This boldness empowers you to confront challenges and fulfill your mission each day.

Consider your fears and anxieties. What is holding you back from addressing these issues? It could be a conflict with a boss, a challenging situation at work, or a difficult relationship. Whatever it is, identifying the source of your avoidance is the first step. Once you've pinpointed the issue, you can create an action plan to address it.

THE POWER OF CONFRONTATION

Confronting what you've been avoiding can be transformative. It could be the key to unlocking a new opportunity, a promotion, or a breakthrough in your life. If you're feeling stuck or trapped in a particular situation or relationship, avoidance might be the root cause.

Don't delay. Take that step forward. Embrace the confidence that God has given you to face these challenges. By confronting what you've been avoiding, you'll set yourself free and move to the next level in your personal or professional life.

Stop avoiding it, and take the bold action needed to move forward!

INTERVENTION

SESSION 16

FORGET THE PAST!

Let's reflect on Isaiah 43:18, which says, *"Do not call to mind former things or ponder things of the past."* One of the most crucial principles for us as women is learning how to let go of the past successfully. The word "forget" implies a sense of loss, as if a memory has faded. Isaiah instructs us not to call to mind former things, meaning we should avoid recalling certain events, situations, or people.

Isaiah's point is significant: when we dwell on past losses, it creates a chain reaction that can alter our behavior, change our patterns, and even sabotage our current beliefs and aspirations. As you read, keep your goal of emotional and spiritual healing in mind.

To embrace the new blessings in your life, you must stop dwelling on past losses. Doing so allows you to open up to fresh perspectives and new opportunities. You will experience new ways of thinking, gain fresh insights about your relationships and daily interactions, and see a positive transformation in all areas of your life. Remember, if you continue to dwell on what has been lost, you risk missing the new things God is doing for you. Move forward by letting go of past regrets and allow yourself to experience the newness awaiting you.

WORKSHEET: FORGET THE PAST!

"Do not call to mind former things or ponder things of the past." – Isaiah 43:18

This session focuses on releasing the weight of past experiences so you can embrace the new blessings God has in store. Use this worksheet to reflect on how past events may be holding you back and explore ways to move forward with renewed faith and purpose.

Part 1: Self-Reflection

1. **Identify Past Regrets**
   - List 3-5 past events, situations, or relationships that you often recall and feel regretful about:

     - _____

     - _____

     - _____

     - _____

     - _____

2. **Impact Assessment**
   - Reflect on how dwelling on these past regrets has affected your present behavior and beliefs:

     - In what ways has it altered your behavior?
       _____

     - Have these memories changed your thought patterns or daily interactions?
       _____

     - How have these regrets impacted your goals or your ability to trust God's plans?
       _____

Part 2: Releasing the Past

1. **Prayer of Release**
   - Write a prayer asking God to help you release these past regrets and open your heart to new opportunities: *Example: "Lord, I release the pain of my past into Your loving hands. Help me to let go of these burdens and trust in the new blessings You have for me."*

   My Prayer:

   _____
   _____
   _____

2. **Gratitude Exercise**

    o Write down three things you are grateful for today. This will help you focus on the present and acknowledge God's blessings:

    1. _____
    2. _____
    3. _____

Part 3: Creating New Patterns

1. **Reframe Your Mindset**

    o How can you shift your thoughts from dwelling on the past to embracing the present? Write down a positive affirmation that will help you stay focused on today's blessings: *Example: "I am open to God's new opportunities and trust in His perfect timing."*

    My Affirmation:

    _____

    _____

2. **Action Steps for Letting Go**

    o List 2-3 actionable steps you can take this week to move forward and let go of past regrets:

    1. _____

2. _____

3. _____

Part 4: Reflection Questions

1. **New Insights**
   - What new perspectives or insights have you gained from letting go of past losses?

   _____
   _____

2. **Transformation Goals**
   - How do you expect your life to change as you embrace the new blessings God has for you?

   _____
   _____

Remember: Letting go of the past is a journey. Be patient with yourself and trust that God is doing a new thing in your life. Isaiah 43:18 reminds us that holding onto old memories can prevent us from seeing the beautiful plans He has for our future. Choose to release, trust, and walk forward in faith.

Take your time to work through each section and revisit this worksheet whenever you need to renew your commitment to letting go.

SESSION 17

THE MORE YOU COMPROMISE, THE LESS COMPATIBLE YOU ARE!

This session's principle stems from a lesson I learned years ago. I was watching Bishop Noel Jones speak to a group of single people about the dangers of compromise in relationships. He shared how compromise can either strengthen or weaken our connections. The takeaway was simple but powerful: *the more you compromise, the less compatible you become with someone or something.*

Compromise means reaching a settlement where both sides make concessions. However, when applied to your values and beliefs, compromise means settling in ways that contradict your core self. As I mentioned in the first chapter, we each have a set of beliefs and values. When you start compromising these fundamental aspects, you become less in harmony with who you truly are.

In relationships, the key is to recognize where you've compromised. Being compatible means living in harmony. If you've found yourself in chaos or pain, it might be due to compromising your values. To reclaim your peace, take inventory of your life. Reflect on relationships, jobs, or situations where you compromised your beliefs. Write them down and examine how long you've been compromising and why.

This is a process of self-intervention. Be honest with yourself about how you came to settle for things that don't align with your core beliefs. Confront these issues lovingly, remembering Ephesians 4:15, which encourages us to speak the truth in love.

This illustration depicts a scale, with "Core Values" on one side and "Compromises" on the other. It visually demonstrates how each decision affects your sense of integrity and the harmony of your relationships.

Compromise and Compatibility Scale

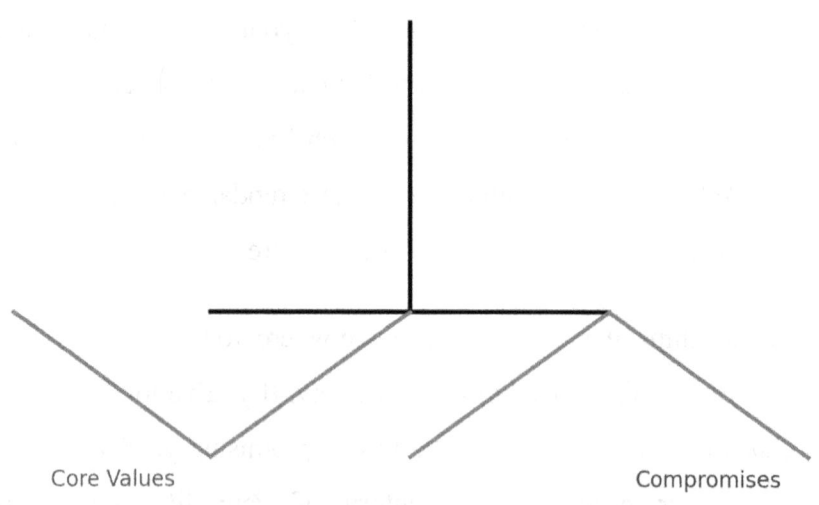

WORKSHEET: THE MORE YOU COMPROMISE, THE LESS COMPATIBLE YOU ARE!

Session 17: Reflecting on Compromise and Compatibility

This session focuses on understanding how compromising your values and beliefs can lead to disharmony in your relationships and life. Use this worksheet to assess where you have compromised and to take steps toward reclaiming your core values and peace.

Part 1: Understanding Compromise

1. **Definition Reflection**
   - In your own words, define what compromise means when it comes to your values and beliefs:

   _____
   _____

2. **Core Values Identification**
   - List 3-5 of your most important core values. These are principles that guide your actions and decisions:

     1. _____
     2. _____
     3. _____
     4. _____
     5. _____

Part 2: Recognizing Compromise

1. **Where Have You Compromised?**

    o Reflect on areas in your life where you have made compromises that contradicted your core beliefs. This could be in relationships, jobs, or other significant areas:

    ■ Situation 1: _____

    ■ Situation 2: _____

    ■ Situation 3: _____

2. **Impact Assessment**

    o How did compromising your values make you feel in the long run? Did it bring you peace, or did it create chaos and pain? Describe the impact:

    _____
    _____

3. **Duration and Reasons**

    o How long have you been compromising in these areas, and what motivated you to settle? Was it fear, a desire to please, or something else?

    _____
    _____
    _____

Part 3: Self-Intervention

1. **Confronting the Issues**

    o Ephesians 4:15 says, "Speak the truth in love." Take a moment to lovingly confront yourself about these compromises. Write a letter to yourself addressing the areas where you've settled: *Example: "Dear Self, I know you compromised your happiness to avoid conflict, but it's time to honor your core values."*

    My Letter:

    _____
    _____
    _____

2. **Speaking the Truth in Love**

    o Practice stating your core beliefs and values firmly but lovingly. Write down a declaration that affirms your commitment to living in harmony with your true self: *Example: "I will no longer compromise my values for the sake of temporary peace. I am worthy of relationships and opportunities that align with who I am."*

    My Declaration:

    _____
    _____
    _____

Part 4: Reclaiming Your Peace

1. **Inventory of Relationships and Situations**
   - Make a list of relationships, jobs, or commitments you need to reassess because they may not align with your core values:

     1. _____
     2. _____
     3. _____

2. **Steps to Reclaim Harmony**
   - List 2-3 actionable steps you can take to begin aligning your life with your values. These might include having an honest conversation, setting new boundaries, or seeking new opportunities:

     1. _____
     2. _____
     3. _____

Part 5: Reflection Questions

1. **What Have You Learned?**
   - What insights have you gained about the impact of compromise on your life and well-being?

     _____
     _____

2. **Future Commitments**

    o How do you plan to uphold your values moving forward and ensure that you remain compatible with your true self?

    _____
    _____
    _____

Remember: Compromising your values might seem easier in the short term, but it often leads to long-term discomfort and dissatisfaction. Honor your beliefs and make choices that reflect your true self. Speak the truth in love, both to yourself and others, and commit to living a life that aligns with who God created you to be.

This chart provides a space for you to map out where compromises have led to a misalignment with your true self. It encourages you to reflect on these choices and consider how to realign with your core values.

Compromise	Impact on Compatibility
Ignored red flags	Loss of trust
Settled for less than I deserve	Increased dissatisfaction
Changed core beliefs to please others	Decreased sense of self-worth

Take time to work through this worksheet, and revisit it whenever you need to remind yourself of your worth and the importance of living in harmony with your values.

SESSION 18

SUITABLE AND COMPATIBLE!

Building on the previous session, this principle focuses on understanding what is "suitable and compatible." After realizing where I had compromised, I had to admit my mistakes. I had to acknowledge that I had formed agreements with situations and people that contradicted my core values. I realized that many of these relationships weren't fulfilling or Godly.

As I sought healing, I asked God, "What is suitable and compatible with who I am now?" The word "suitable" means adapted or appropriate for a specific purpose or person. I began to focus on seeking what was truly suitable for my life, not just on who or what I encountered.

This principle extends to every area of life, including relationships. I prayed, "God, bring me what is appropriate for where I am." Even in my marriage, when facing conflicts, I pray for the suitable and compatible response. Years ago, when praying for a life partner, I asked God to send someone suitable.

Suitable and Compatible!

"Compatible" means existing in harmony. True compatibility allows us to live and work together peacefully, aligned with our core selves. By asking God for what is suitable and compatible, we invite relationships and opportunities that align with our purpose. The more we compromise, the more we distance ourselves from our true selves. Shedding these compromises allows us to live authentically.

Pray with intention: *God, bring into my life the person, place, or opportunity that is appropriate and harmonious with my true self.*

SESSION 19

RENEWING YOUR MIND!

In this session, we will discuss the importance of renewing your mind. Romans 12:1-2 provides timeless wisdom that can transform your life:

1. *"I beseech you, therefore, brethren, by the mercies of God, that you present your bodies a living sacrifice, holy and acceptable to God, which is your reasonable service."*

2. *"And do not be conformed to this world but be transformed by the renewing of your mind, that you may prove what is good and acceptable and the perfect will of God."*

To experience true transformation, you must be willing to renew your mind entirely through God's Word. This process is not just about a measurable, quantitative change but about a qualitative transformation—a new and higher quality of life and thinking. When we compromise, we diminish our authentic selves and settle for less than what God has for us.

Renewing your mind is an exchange: letting go of old, unproductive ways of thinking and embracing the new. For single women waiting for God to bring the right partner, it means seeking a person of quality, someone who matches the standards and values you uphold. If you've experienced past relationships that didn't work out, ask yourself if they were truly compatible. Remember, this doesn't devalue the other person; they simply weren't the right fit for you.

Years before I got married, a prophetic word declared that my future mate would be "like a hand in a glove, suitable and compatible." This gave me guidance and patience. The goal is to find joy, peace, and people who are compatible with who you are at your core. Allow this renewal to transform your life, elevate your thinking, and guide you into relationships and opportunities of higher quality.

This mind map shows how your thinking can be transformed. It branches out into "Old Thoughts" and "New Thoughts," illustrating how a renewed mindset can lead to different and more positive life outcomes.

Mind Renewal Mind Map

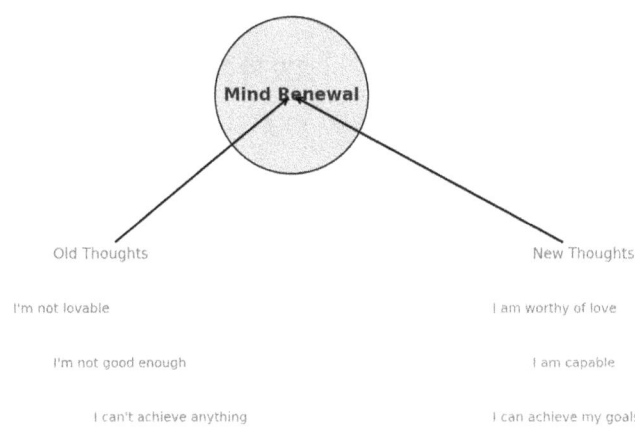

REFLECTION QUESTIONS:
SESSION 19 - RENEWING YOUR MIND!

Use these questions to reflect on the process of renewing your mind and aligning your thoughts and actions with God's will for your life. Romans 12:1-2 emphasizes the importance of not conforming to the world but experiencing transformation through the renewal of your mind. Take time to answer these thoughtfully, focusing on how this transformation can lead to a higher quality of life and relationships.

1. **Understanding Transformation**

    o What does "renewing your mind" mean to you in the context of Romans 12:1-2?

    _____
    _____
    _____

2. **Letting Go of Old Thinking Patterns**

    o Identify three unproductive or negative thought patterns that have held you back. How have these thoughts impacted your life and decisions?

    1. _____
    2. _____
    3. _____

3. **The Exchange Process**

    o   What new, God-honoring thoughts or beliefs do you need to embrace to experience true transformation?

    _____
    _____
    _____
    _____

4. **Reflecting on Past Relationships**

    o   Think about a past relationship that didn't work out. Were there signs that the person was not compatible with your values and standards? If so, what were they?

    _____
    _____
    _____
    _____

5. **Compatibility and Standards**

    o   What standards and values do you uphold that are essential for compatibility in a future partner? How do you intend to stay true to these without compromise?

    _____
    _____
    _____
    _____

6. **Patience and Guidance**
   - Reflect on a time when you felt God's guidance, whether through Scripture, a prophetic word, or a sense of peace. How did that experience influence your patience and trust in God's timing?

   _____
   _____
   _____

7. **The Hand-in-Glove Analogy**
   - The analogy of a future mate being "like a hand in a glove" speaks to a perfect, comfortable fit. What does this imagery mean to you, and how does it shape your vision for a future relationship?

   _____
   _____
   _____

8. **Higher Quality of Life and Relationships**
   - How does the idea of a "qualitative transformation" inspire you to seek joy, peace, and relationships that are in harmony with who you are at your core?

   _____
   _____
   _____

9. **Areas for Renewing Your Mind**

    o In which areas of your life (relationships, career, self-worth, spiritual walk) do you feel most called to renew your mind? Why are these areas significant to your overall well-being?

    _____
    _____
    _____
    _____

10. **Moving Forward with Renewed Thinking**

    o What specific actions will you take to ensure that your mind is continually being renewed by God's Word? How can you incorporate daily practices like prayer, meditation, or Scripture study into your routine?

    _____
    _____
    _____

This before-and-after chart outlines the potential impact of renewing your mind on various areas of life, such as your relationships, career, and self-esteem, demonstrating how positive thinking can bring about significant change.

Area of Life	Old Thoughts	New Thoughts
Relationships	I'm not lovable	I am worthy of love and healthy relationships
Career	I'm not good enough for this job	I am capable and deserving of career success
Self-Esteem	I can't achieve anything meaningful	I am empowered and can achieve my goals

Final Thoughts

Remember, renewing your mind is a continual journey, not a one-time event. Each day presents an opportunity to exchange old, limiting beliefs for God's truth, elevating your thinking and guiding you toward the abundant life He has planned for you. Use these reflections to deepen your spiritual growth and align your actions with God's perfect will.

SESSION 20

MAKING DECISIONS

This session focuses on motivating yourself to incorporate the principles of Healing H.E.R. into your life. If you're asking, *"How do I get started on this healing journey?"* or *"How can I internalize these concepts?"*, I have an exercise that can help.

Using the acronym **D.A.R.N.**—which stands for Desire, Ability, Reason, and Need—you can measure your readiness for change. On a piece of paper, draw a horizontal line from 1 to 10, with 1 being the lowest and 10 the highest. Use this scale to rate yourself in four areas:

- **Desire**: How strong is your desire to make a change?
- **Ability**: How capable do you feel of making this change?
- **Reason**: Why is it important to change?
- **Need**: How urgent is this change in your life?

For example, if you're thinking about buying a car, you might rate your desire at 7, your ability at 3, your reason at 7, and your need at 2. If your scores vary widely, it may not be the right time to make that decision. Generally, it's best to act when your scores for Desire, Ability, Reason, and Need are all above 5.

Change Talk, based on Miller & Rollnick's principles, emphasizes that the more you talk about making a change, the more likely you are to follow through. The mnemonic **DARN-CAT** can guide your self-reflection:

- **Desire**: "I want to change."
- **Ability**: "I can change."
- **Reason**: "It's important to change."
- **Need**: "I should change."
- **Commitment**: "I will change."
- **Activation**: "I am ready to change."
- **Taking Steps**: "I am taking action to change."

TERMINATION

SESSION 21

LET GO OF WHAT DOESN'T CHANGE!

This session addresses behaviors and thought patterns that are either productive or counterproductive. A core principle here is *termination*, which means ending or letting go of what no longer serves you. To grow and transform, you must let go of stagnant relationships, mindsets, and habits.

The most important relationship is with God, followed by your relationship with yourself. Both should involve continuous growth. Change is a constant, and you must confront areas of your life that hinder your progress. For this session's exercise, create a two-column list:

1. **Productive**: Write down people, decisions, and relationships that have positively impacted your life. Categorize them into mentality, emotions, finances, and relationships.

2. **Counterproductive**: List things or people that have been unhelpful or harmful. Consider the same categories.

Reflect on your list and ask yourself if these elements align with your core values. God desires a better-quality life for you, and part of this journey is embracing new thoughts and motivations that elevate your spirit. Letting go of counterproductive influences may be difficult, but it's crucial for emotional and spiritual growth. Be honest about how these things have affected you and be willing to let God guide you through this process of renewal.

SESSION 22

KNOWING IT BY THE FRUIT!

This session builds on the previous principle of letting go of things that do not change. The next key concept is to "Know it by the fruit." Here, "fruit" can refer to thoughts, ideas, or behaviors that emerged due to a specific situation or relationship. To assess this, refer back to the sheet with two columns you created in the last session.

Review the items you listed and ask yourself:

- What are the outcomes of your financial decisions?
- How are your current thoughts and mental state affecting you?
- Are your thoughts and behaviors leading to productivity or causing stress, anxiety, or even depression?

Answering these questions, along with the ones from the previous session, will bring clarity to what is productive and what needs to be terminated. This session is about identifying and confronting non-productive areas. If you notice that certain things on your list have negative fruit, it is time to consider weeding them out. Start with the top 3 to 5 items that emotionally and spiritually drain you.

Ask yourself: *"What has been the result of this?"* If the fruit isn't healthy or productive, then it may be time to change that behavior or let go of that influence. Closure and termination are not the end but rather opportunities to move forward. Do not fear these processes, but instead, use wisdom to know and remove unproductive influences in your life.

SESSION 23

THE WALK-THROUGH! (PART 1)

This session introduces the "walk-through" concept, which will be expanded over four parts. The walk-through principle is about assessing and possibly terminating relationships, behaviors, or patterns in your life using the **D.A.R.N.** framework: Desire, Ability, Reason, and Need.

Imagine you are looking for an apartment or house. You do a walk-through to see if it meets your needs, understand its costs, and determine its strengths and weaknesses. Similarly, in life, we do walk-throughs when considering new relationships, ideas, or commitments. We must also do walk-throughs when evaluating if something should be maintained or terminated.

When terminating a relationship:

- **Desire**: Communicate your desire to end or change the relationship.
- **Ability**: Evaluate if you have the ability to sustain the relationship healthily.

The Walk-Through! (Part 1)

- **Reason**: Explain why the relationship needs to change or end.
- **Need**: Determine what you require to move forward.

Write down your thoughts and use this process to gain clarity and confidence. Practicing this will prepare you for real-life scenarios. Be honest and gentle with yourself as you explore internal factors and habits that you want to change. Visualizing and meditating on your ability to make changes is crucial.

This flowchart guides you step-by-step through evaluating your emotions, relationships, and behaviors. It includes visual checkpoints where you can decide what aspects of your life to keep and what to let go of.

Walk-Through Concept Flowchart

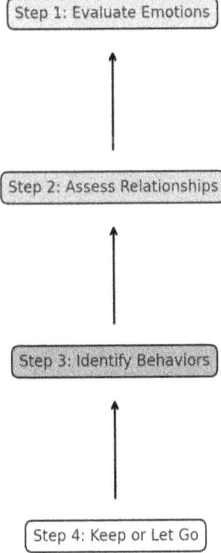

For example, if someone wants to quit smoking, they would ask:

- What is my desire to stop?
- What is my ability to quit?
- What are my reasons for wanting to change?
- What is my need to make this change?

If these questions aren't answered clearly, no change will occur. Use the D.A.R.N. principle, combined with the 1-10 scale, to objectively assess your motivation and readiness to change. Visualize Proverbs 23:7: *"As a man thinks in his heart, so is he."* The walk-through helps you identify and terminate non-productive patterns and relationships, bringing you closer to becoming your best self.

SESSION 24

THE WALK-THROUGH! (PART 2)

We continue with the walk-through principle, focusing on follow-up and termination in relationships and personal behaviors. Visualize yourself walking through your life, similar to how you'd assess a new home. Doing this exercise helps you determine if certain aspects of your life are in alignment with your goals and well-being.

Try a 30-second visualization:

- What do you notice in your emotional life?
- How does your mental health feel during the walk-through?
- What do you observe in your financial or spiritual state?

Close your eyes and reflect honestly. Speak the truth to yourself in love, as advised in Ephesians 4:15. What things should remain? What needs to be eliminated?

Philippians 3:14 says: *"I press toward the mark for the prize of the high calling of God in Christ Jesus."* The Apostle Paul assumed he had done the work needed to let go of the past. He had endured hardships, betrayals, and disappointments but chose to focus on moving forward. To do the same, we must put in the emotional, mental, and spiritual effort to leave behind the things that hold us back.

This diagram presents a floor plan of a house, with each room representing a different area of your life, like "Emotional Space" or "Mental Space." It helps you assess and organize your personal and emotional well-being.

Walk-Through Concept House Floor Plan

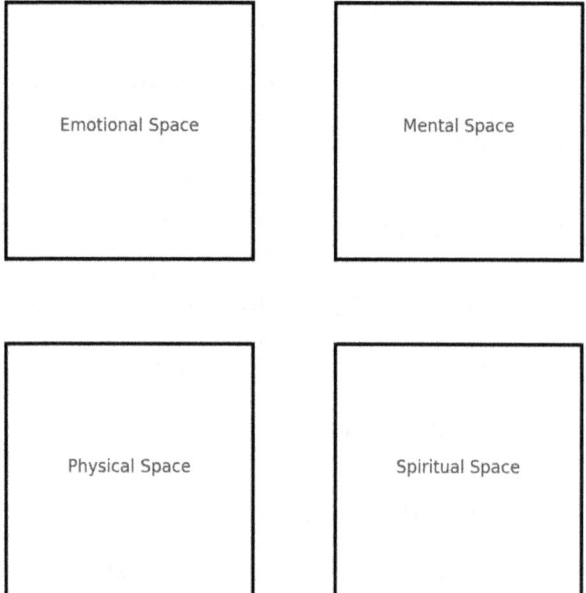

Termination doesn't mean erasing memories but letting go of the emotional hold certain experiences have over you. The Apostle Paul

The Walk-Through! (Part 2)

reached a point where he was ready to move on, and we must be willing to do the same. As you assess your life, consider these three areas:

- Emotions: Address negative feelings and memories with professional guidance.
- Mental Walk-Through: Visualize the changes you need to make and how they will benefit you.
- Taking Care of Yourself: Make decisions that prioritize your well-being.

Reflect on what needs to be released. What do you experience when you mentally walk through your life? Address these areas so you can press forward, just as Paul did.

SESSION 25

THE WALK-THROUGH! (PART 3)

This is the third of four sessions focused on the topic of "The Walk-Through." In the previous session, we discussed Philippians 3:12-14, where the Apostle Paul urges us to forget the things behind us. "Forget" here means to lose or neglect, and Paul emphasizes letting go of emotions, relationships, and traditions that no longer have a positive impact on our lives. By doing so, we gain the ability to press forward.

Paul reminds us that holding on to the past creates a struggle to move forward. Neglecting the past allows us to direct our attention to what lies ahead. During your walk-through, ask yourself: *What emotions or memories trigger you?* Once you identify these triggers, visualize yourself moving away from them.

Joshua 1:8 speaks about meditating on God's word. Meditation is like creating something new, just as baking a cake requires ingredients. Your new thoughts, ideas, emotions, and mindsets should replace the old ones. If you realize that what you initially desired isn't what you want anymore, revisit the **D.A.R.N.** principle: Desire, Ability, Reason, and Need.

Paul's motivation came from what lay ahead. Do the same for your walk-through. Take five minutes each day to reflect, identify what you need to leave behind, and focus on creating new memories and beliefs. Purge anything that no longer serves you, including people who shouldn't have exclusive access to your life.

I am passionate about self-intimacy and want you to confidently use these sessions to heal and become whole. Ask yourself: *Does anyone want what I have to offer?* Be confident that with God and your gifts, you can be a problem-solver for others. Take your walk-through and know that your life is being transformed for the better.

FOLLOWING UP

SESSION 26

THE WALK-THROUGH! (PART 4)

We continue with Philippians 3:12-14, focusing on the concept of maturity. Paul says, "Not that I have already attained or am already perfected, but I press on." The word "perfected" here means to mature. Maturity involves making responsible and accountable decisions.

Paul uses maturity to signify an arrival at a place of accountability and growth. As you walk through your life, you will see new opportunities and relationships that you are now mature enough to handle. Maturity allows you to leave behind mediocrity and pursue what aligns with your values.

Paul encourages us to leave past hindrances behind. As you think about your walk-through, recognize that past beliefs or situations were simply what you could handle at the time. Let go of old triggers and see them for what they were: moments of growth or lessons learned.

The Walk-Through! (Part 4)

Decide today what you want to be part of your new life. Understand that you create your beliefs, and it starts now. Your walk-through should guide you toward behaviors and thoughts rooted in God's word. Just as you might renovate a house, your life can be remodeled and improved.

Remember, the walk-through is a vital tool for achieving a better quality of life. You have the power to create a renewed, purposeful existence.

SESSION 27

FOLLOW UP WITH FAVOR!

In this session, we focus on the concept of following up with favor. Favor means an attitude of approval or an act of kindness beyond what is due. I learned this principle from my mother, who, as a customer service director, inspired others to go above and beyond in their service.

My mother's approach to life taught me to command favor confidently. People often showed her kindness, and she would follow up, building lasting relationships. Who in your life has shown you favor? Can you follow up with them to build on that connection? This practice will help you establish boundaries and reinforce positive principles.

Luke 6:45 says, "Out of the abundance of your heart flows the issues of life." When your thinking aligns with favor, your behavior will reflect it. Be aware of double-mindedness, which James 1:5 warns against. Double-mindedness, or vacillation, can prevent you from fully embracing the favor God and people show you. Choose a course of action and stick to it.

Do not doubt the principles you've learned. Practice favor by being kind beyond what is expected, both to others and to yourself. Recognize that favor comes from consistency and integrity. Build relationships with those who have supported you, and be mindful of people who may only want to benefit from your favor.

Following up with favor leads to more opportunities and blessings. Be intentional about nurturing these relationships, and remember to extend the same favor to yourself. Within the next few months, make it a point to follow up with those who have shown you kindness and support.

SESSION 28

ADMIRING VS. HONORING

This session covers the principle of admiration versus honoring. While both involve respect, there's a significant difference between the two. The term "admire" means to regard with respect and to think highly of someone. "Honor," on the other hand, implies high respect, privilege, or a greater level of respect.

Consider how you would treat a figure like President Obama compared to a teacher. Both deserve respect, but the level of honor differs. This session invites you to reflect on the codes, laws, or regulations surrounding the people in your life and the level of honor you give yourself. Do you present yourself in a way that commands admiration or honor?

Here are four questions you can ask others to discern if someone is worth honoring or just admiring:

1. What do I need to do to reach your level of success?
2. How can you help me achieve my goal?
3. When did you realize you would be successful?

4. How did you get to where you are?

If someone struggles to provide meaningful answers to these questions, they may be worth admiring but not necessarily honoring. Those worthy of honor will have significant insights to share and can help you reach your goals. Their willingness to mentor and guide you is a mark of their worthiness.

People you honor should have a clear pattern of success and not hesitate to share their wisdom. Honor propels you to the next level, beyond where you are currently. Remember, honor involves more than admiration; it involves learning from and respecting someone who has something meaningful to impart.

SESSION 29

KEEP DEFINING YOURSELF

In this session, titled "Keep Defining Yourself," you'll be asked to reflect on five self-evaluation questions. These questions are crucial for centering yourself and ensuring you're nurturing your needs. It's easy to neglect yourself while taking care of everyone else, but this exercise will help bring you back to a healthy place.

Here are the five questions for self-evaluation:

1. What are the three things that make the most significant difference in your life?
2. What are the three things that give you pure joy?
3. What does success mean to you at this stage of your life?
4. What three things are you working to complete?
5. What are your three core rules (emotionally, physically, spiritually, and financially)?

Answering these questions will help you thrive and recognize the kind of relationships that can support your well-being. Self-evaluation is a powerful tool to ensure you are living in alignment with your values and goals.

SESSION 30

THREE KEYS TO HEALING H.E.R.

As we conclude this series, we focus on the three keys to healing:

1. **Love Yourself**
2. **Deal with Trauma**
3. **Do the Work to Heal**

Healing is a journey, and it doesn't happen overnight. There are moments of sudden realization, but some wounds take years to heal. Be patient with yourself. Healing is a spiritual process that is unique to each individual, but these three keys are universal.

The first step is to **love yourself**. Commit to loving yourself even if no one else does. Believe in your purpose and what God has called you to do. Find out who you are through God's word and other resources.

Next, **deal with any trauma**. Trauma doesn't just disappear; it often roots itself within you. Identify your disappointments and figure out how they are impacting your life. Unresolved trauma can lead to discontentment and diminish your capacity to trust or love.

Finally, **do the necessary work to heal**. Healing requires action. Whether it's through counseling, mentorship, or studying resources, you must put in the effort. Healing involves reaching out and finding guidance from trusted individuals. Remember, faith without works is dead (James 2:14).

Healing involves taking responsibility for your life and doing the work to bring about positive change. Reflect on the sessions that resonated most with you, and revisit them to understand the steps you need to take. You have the tools and principles; now, it's time to apply them. Proverbs 4:7 says, "In all thy getting, get an understanding." Understanding leads to a life full of health and growth.

What next? Join the Healing H.E.R. program, curated by Amethyst Roberson, MA LPC, is a transformative journey aimed at empowering women through Healing, Empowerment, and Restoration. This comprehensive initiative is grounded in the wisdom of the Bible and evidence-based practices, designed to guide participants through structured stages and principles to foster profound, personal growth and healing. Here's a glimpse into the expected outcomes of the critical components of the program: **Go to amethystroberson.com**

A SYSTEM OF HEALING, EMPOWERMENT & RESTORATION
6 PRACTICES & 30 COMMITMENTS

RELATIONSHIP
- You Create your own belief system
- You have to believe that God thinks well of you
- Get wisdom
- Perception is everything
- Anything you allow will increase

ASSESSMENT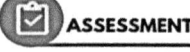
- You can solve whatever problems you see
- Is anyone in need of you
- Discern your encouragers
- Find the root of your pain
- Receive consolation for your soul

GOALS
- You have what someone else is mission
- Confidence part I
- Confidence part II
- What is the source of your worth
- Stop avoid it

INTERVENTION
- Forget the past
- The more you compromise the less compatible you are
- Suitable and compatible
- Renew your mind
- Motivate yourself

TERMINATION
- Let go of what doesn't change
- Know it by the fruit
- The walk through
- The walk through part 2
- The walk through part 3

FOLLOW UP
- The walk through part 4
- Follow up with favor
- Admiration vs Honoring
- Keep Defining Yourself
- 3 keys to healing

REFERENCES

1. Bishop Noel Jones- "The More you compromise, the less compatible you are" (Sermon)

2. https://www.5lovelanguages.com/

3. Motivational Interviewing: Helping People Change. Guilford Press, 2013.

4. Hetzendorfer, Ruth. The Pastoral Counseling Handbook: a Guide to Helping the Hurting. Beacon Hill Press of Kansas City, 2009.

5. All scripture references retrieved from https://biblehub.com/kjv/

6. goodtherapy.org

7. Dictionary.com

8. www.therelationshipinstitute.org

9. Change Talk (Miller & Rollnick, 2013)

www.ingramcontent.com/pod-product-compliance
Lightning Source LLC
Chambersburg PA
CBHW050648160426
43194CB00010B/1860